P9-CLB-301

Mark Breslin's

INTERNATIONAL · STAND · UP COMEDY

TM FUNNY BUSINESS PRODUCTIONS INC.

Jokes

MEN ONLY

TELL Other MEN

Compiled and edited by
Jeff Silverman and Lawrence Morgenstern
Illustrated by Dave Cornell

ECW Press

NATIONAL LIBRARY OF CANADA CATALOGUING IN PUBLICATION DATA

Yuk Yuk's joke books

Contents: v. 1. Classic Jokes. — v. 2. Jokes for roasts and toasts.
— v. 3. Jokes men only tell other men.

ISBN 1-55022-606-1 (v. 1.).— ISBN — 1-55022-605-3 (v. 2.).
ISBN 1-55022-607-X (v. 3.).

1. Wit and humor. I. Yuk Yuk's (Toronto, Ont.)

PN6151.Y84 2003   808.87   C2003-902184-X

Cover and Text Design: Tania Craan
Printing: Transcontinental

This book is set in Imago

DISTRIBUTION
CANADA: Jaguar Book Group, 100 Armstrong Avenue, Georgetown, on L7G 5S4

UNITED STATES: Independent Publishers Group, 814 North Franklin Street,
Chicago, Illinois 60610

PRINTED AND BOUND IN CANADA

ECW PRESS
ecwpress.com

**Yuk Yuk's "On Tour" offers all types of comedic entertainment for any
occasion. From major concerts to company parties we deliver the laughs.
Call: Funny Business East: 416-967-6431 Ext. 246
or Funny Business West 403-258-2040.**

PREFACE

They're crude, tasteless, vulgar, obscene, and offensive. But enough about Pamela Anderson's hot tub parties; let's discuss the jokes in this book. You are holding one in a series of official Yuk Yuk's joke books. That's right. The organization that brought you stand-up comedy in malls and tap water in Evian bottles proudly presents a bold new frontier in publishing and revenue generation. It's our hope that you, the general public, are enlightened, amused, and entertained by these books and, more importantly, that you buy them before they hit the remainder bins.

A brief word of caution about this volume. The material contained here is extremely mature in nature. Which basically means there's a lot of stuff about doing it and women accidentally becoming naked. Now, while for reasons of aplomb and tact, the *peepee* and *poopoo* words do not appear in this foreword, they are in abundance throughout the rest of this volume and are even part of people's surnames.

Great care was taken in gathering only the finest and most disgusting bon mots for this volume. We went through thousands of gags and eliminated those that seemed old hat or forced. We weeded out jokes that seemed to have no basis in reality. While it's true that a girl who lets you have your way with her and then turns into a pizza and a six-pack is an ideal date, it's probably unlikely to ever happen.

What was left now resides in the following pages. If you like a ribald laugh, chances are you'll like the jests here. And, with any luck, you'll have already heard only about sixty to seventy percent of them. Read them, share them, enjoy them. But, for God's sake, don't let your mother find them.

Why is there a head on your dick?
To keep your hand
from sliding off.

Two whores are walking down the street, and one says, "I smell cock."
The other one replies, "Sorry. I just burped."

Why does a dog lick his balls?
Because he can't make a fist.

What's the difference between a blonde and a brick?
You can lay a brick only once.

Did you hear about the lady golfer who was hit by a ball between the first and second holes?
She had a hell of a time putting the Band-Aid on.

How can you tell if a girl is a redneck?
She blows you while chewing tobacco and knows what to spit out and what to swallow.

A little girl asks her mother, "Mommy, where do babies come from?"

"Well, honey," answers the mother, "when a man and a woman love each other, they have sex. That's when a man puts his penis in the woman's vagina. After that they get a baby."

"But Mommy, last night I saw you put Daddy's penis in your mouth. What does that get you?"

"Jewelry."

How do you know when you're enjoying
a porno film?
You butter your own popcorn.

Why don't blondes breast-feed?
It hurts too much to boil their nipples.

Can a woman get pregnant from anal sex?
Sure. Where do you think lawyers come from?

Where do men stand when it comes to
masturbation?
The shower.

What's the difference between a mashed potato
and pussy?
A mashed potato can't make its own gravy.

How did the blonde get blisters on her lips?
From trying to blow out the lightbulb.

Arnold is fucking his big fat wife when the phone rings. He answers it and says, "Let me call you back. I'm in the tub."

After getting smashed at a party for his boss, a guy asked his wife the next morning, "What happened last night?"

"Well, as usual, you made an ass of yourself in front of your boss," she told him.

"Piss on him," said the guy.

"You did, and he fired you," replied his wife.

"Well, fuck him, then."

"I did. You've been rehired with a raise."

What's the difference between having sex with your wife and having Jell-O? Jell-O wiggles when you eat it.

What's the definition of an 11?
A 10 that swallows.

How can you tell
if your date's horny?
She throws off her panties,
and they stick to the wall.

How can you tell if a woman is
experienced?
She knows when not to cough.

**What do a bleached blonde and a 747
have in common?
They both have a black box.**

What's the smartest thing that ever came
out of a woman's mouth?
Einstein's dick.

Two bums are walking through the red-light district when a hooker comes up and asks them, "Hey, guys, does either one of you want a hand job?"

"Uh, no thanks," mutters the first bum.

A little while later, they pass another hooker, who asks them, "Hey, boys, can I interest you in a blow job?"

"Thanks, but no thanks," says the second bum.

After the hooker walks away, the first bum turns to the second bum and says, "Let's go back downtown. We've been here less than 10 minutes, and we've been offered two jobs already."

What's a 68?
You blow me, and I'll owe you one.

A boy and his date are parked on a back road necking when the girl says, "I really should have mentioned this earlier, but I'm actually a hooker, and I charge $50 for sex."

The boy reluctantly pays her, and they continue. After they're done, the boy just looks out the driver's window.

"Why aren't we going anywhere?" she asks him.

"Well, I should have mentioned this before, but I'm a cab driver, and the fare back to town is $75."

A lesbian is being examined by her doctor. The doctor says, "My, you have a clean vagina."
The lesbian says, "Thanks, I have a lady come in twice a week."

How is a blonde like a turtle?
Once they're on their backs, they're pretty much fucked.

On their wedding night, a groom confessed to his new bride, "Honey, I think you should know I'm a total golf nut. You'll never see me on weekends during the golf season."

"I have a confession too, dear," she said quietly. "I'm a hooker."

"Hey, no big deal," said the groom. "Just keep your head down and your arm straight."

A man and a blonde are making out in his car when he asks her, "Do you want to move to the back seat?"

To which she replies, "Oh no, I want to stay here in the front with you."

Did you hear about the ugly kid at camp? He jerked off so much he had to fold his sheets with a hammer.

What do the Bermuda Triangle and a blonde have in common?
They've both swallowed a lot of seamen.

Why do blondes wear panties?
They make good ankle warmers.

Why don't pygmies use tampons?
They keep tripping on the strings.

What's a Polish ménage à trois?
Using two hands to jerk off.

How do you make a woman scream twice?
Fuck her in the ass and then wipe your dick
on her curtains.

What did one gerbil say to the other gerbil?
"Let's go to Richard Gere's house and get
shitfaced."

Why do blondes like tilt steering?
More headroom.

What are the five worst things about being a dick?

1. You have only one eye.
2. Your owner is always choking you.
3. Your neighbors are two nuts and an asshole.
4. Your best friend is a cunt.
5. The party is always over just when you come.

Why do women have two sets of lips? So they can piss and moan at the same time?

What's the difference between a woman and a refrigerator? A refrigerator doesn't fart when you pull your meat out.

An old man goes into the drugstore and asks for Viagra pills, but he wants them cut into fours. "They won't do you much good in such small doses," the pharmacist tells him.

"That's all right," says the old man. "At my age, I don't want 'em for sex. I just want it to stick out far enough so I don't pee on my shoes."

What do women and dog shit have in common?
The older they get, the easier they are to pick up.

How does a blonde hold her liquor?
By the ears.

What's the most common line in a gay bar?
"Is this ass taken?"

One day little Johnny saw his mother naked in the shower and noticed her breasts. Later that day he asked his father, "Daddy, what are those things on Mommy's chest?"

Thinking quickly, Johnny's father said, "Those are Mommy's balloons, Johnny. When she dies, we can blow them up, and she'll float to heaven."

The next day Johnny's father came home from work a few hours early, and Johnny came running out crying hysterically. "Daddy, Daddy, Mommy's dying!"

"Take it easy, Johnny. Why do you think Mommy is dying?"

"The mailman is blowing up her balloons, and she's screaming, 'Oh God, I'm coming!'"

What's the difference between a woman and a toilet?
A toilet doesn't follow you around after you drop your load into it.

What does a blonde's boss say to her as she gets up to leave his office?
"Be sure not to bump your head on the desk."

What did the insecure gay guy say to his lover?
"Does this dildo make my ass look fat?"

A newlywed couple are getting ready for their honeymoon. When the bride undresses in front of her husband for the first time, he asks her, "Can I take a picture of you?"

"Why?" she asks.

"So I can keep it next to my heart," he tells her.

Then the groom gets undressed in front of his bride for the first time. She takes one look at him and asks, "Can I take a picture of you too?"

"Why?" he asks.

"So I can get it enlarged."

A really conceited guy is banging a really conceited girl.
She says, "Aren't I tight?"
He says, "No, just full."

A guy walks into a clock shop and puts his penis on the counter.

The lady behind the counter tells him, "This is a *clock* shop, not a cock shop."

So the guy says, "Good, put two hands and a face on this."

One evening a man comes home to his apartment all roughed up.

"What happened?" asks his wife.

"I got into a fight with another tenant," the man answers.

"Whatever for?"

"He said he slept with every woman in the building except one."

The woman replies, "I bet it's that snooty Mrs. Van Holt in 4-G."

Why do doctors spank babies when they're born?
To knock the dicks off the dumb ones.

What's the difference between eating pussy and driving in the fog?
When you're eating pussy, you can see the asshole in front of you.

Why do women rub their eyes when they wake up?
Because they don't have balls to scratch.

What did the blonde's dentist say?
"You have the whitest teeth I've ever come across."

How do you make four old ladies say "FUCK!"
Get a fifth one to yell "BINGO!"

What's the difference between a blonde and a mosquito?
A mosquito will stop sucking when you slap it.

What do you call a brain-dead guy with no arms and legs and a 14-inch penis?
"Partially" handicapped.

Why did the guy stop having anal sex with his wife?
Because every night it was the same shit.

The priest says to the mechanic fixing his flat tire, "Are the lug nuts on tight?"
The mechanic says, "Tight as a nun's cunt."
The priest thinks for a moment and says, "Better give 'em another turn."

Why was the blonde given a spot in the orchestra even though she was a terrible piano player?
Because she also sucked at the organ.

**What's the last thing that goes through
a bug's mind when it hits the windshield?
Its asshole.**

A masked man goes into a sperm bank, points
a gun at the woman behind the counter, and
says, "Open the safe."

She says, "You know it's not a real bank. It's
a sperm bank."

"Open the safe, or I'll shoot."

She opens the safe.

He says, "Take out one of the bottles and
drink it."

After the woman opens the bottle and drinks
it, the man takes his mask off, and she sees that
it's her husband.

"There, you see?" he says. "It's not so
difficult, is it?"

**What do two lesbians do when they're
menstruating?
Finger-paint.**

**What do you get when you cross a hooker
with a pit bull?
The last blow job you'll ever get.**

Why do blondes take the pill?
So they know what day it is.

**What's the difference between your dick and
your paycheck?
You don't have to beg your wife to blow your
paycheck.**

What's the definition of misery for a middle-aged
woman?
Borrowing her neighbor's douche bag and
finding her husband's false teeth in it.

**Did you hear about the two lesbians who
were building a house together?
It was all tongue and groove, and there
wasn't a stud in the place.**

Why did Ernie think his father had two dicks?
Because he saw him use a small one to pee out of and a huge one to brush the babysitter's teeth with.

How do you tell a woman with PMS from a woman without PMS?
The one without PMS is being a bitch for no reason.

What did the cannibal do after he dumped his wife?
Wiped his ass.

What's the best way to part a girl's hair?
With your tongue.

Why can't blondes water ski?
Because, whenever they feel it get wet between their legs, they open them.

A lesbian walks into a bar, points to a young girl, and says, "I'll have that 16 year old over there."

The bartender looks at her and says, "Sorry, we don't serve minors to lickers."

What do you call a blonde with two brain cells?
Pregnant.

What did the woman mutter as she crawled over the desert with her douche bag?
"Water and vinegar. Water and vinegar."

Little Johnny's father asked him, "Do you know about the birds and the bees?"

"I don't want to know," little Johnny said, bursting into tears.

Confused, Johnny's father asked him what was wrong.

"Oh, Dad," little Johnny sobbed, "when I was six, I got the 'No Santa' speech. At seven I was told there's no Easter Bunny. At eight I heard there's no Tooth Fairy. Now, if you're going to tell me that grown-ups don't really fuck, I've got nothing to live for."

A kid walks up to his dad and says, "Dad, can I have 20 bucks for a blow job?" His father looks at him and says, "I don't know, son, are you any good?"

What do a pizza delivery man and a gynecologist have in common?
They can both smell it all they want, but they're not allowed to eat it.

**How can you tell if you're in a lesbian bar?
The billiard table doesn't have any balls, and
the cue sticks are vibrating.**

How do you brainwash a blonde?
Hang her upside down and give her an enema.

**How many animals are in a pair of
pantyhose?
Fifteen. Two calves in the legs, 10 piggies in
the feet, one ass in the back, one pussy in
the front, and a dead fish nobody can find.**

Why do hillbillies bang sheep on the edge of
a cliff?
They push back harder.

**What did the blonde say after the cop who
pulled her over whipped out his dick?
"Oh no, not another breathalyzer test."**

What do a pussy eater and a mob informant have in common?
One slip of the tongue and they're both in deep shit.

What's the difference between a blonde virgin and Bigfoot?
Some people claim to have seen Bigfoot.

A woman had her face badly burned in a car accident. The doctor said that the only suitable skin for grafting was from her husband's rear end. After the surgery, the wife's face was even more beautiful than ever. One night she tearfully told her husband, "Darling, I'm so grateful to you. I can't thank you enough for what you did for me."

"Think nothing of it, sweetheart," said the husband. "It's thanks enough every time I see your mother kiss you on the cheek."

Two friends are discussing their love lives. The first guy says, "My wife is always losing interest halfway through sex."

"You should do what I do," says the second guy. "When she gets bored, I fire a starter pistol. She gets so frightened it excites her all over again."

The next week they meet again. "Did you try the starter pistol?" asks the second guy.

"Oh, brother, did I!" says the first guy. "We were in the middle of 69 when I tried it. My wife got so scared she bit my cock and shit on my face, and a guy came out of the closet with his hands up."

What did the blonde's right leg say to the left leg?
Nothing—they've never met.

**What do you get when you cross
a homosexual with a dinosaur?
A Mega-sore-ass.**

What did the bartender whisper to the
lesbian when a bull dyke walked into
the bar?
"She's hung like a doughnut."

**A guy goes into a pharmacy and asks
the girl behind the counter, "Do you
keep stationery?"**

**The girl replies, "Yes, I do, until
someone touches my clit; then I go
crazy."**

What do you get when you
cross a lesbian with a dinosaur?
A Lick-a-lotta-puss.

A man moves to a small rural town, and on his first day there this old guy drives up to him in a pick-up and says, "Welcome to town, neighbor. I got an invitation for you to this big party I'm throwing tonight. There's gonna be drinkin', dancin', fightin', and fuckin'."

"Sounds great," says the man. "What should I wear?"

"Don't matter," says the old man. "It's just gonna be you and me."

How can you tell if a blonde has been in your refrigerator?
By the lipstick on your cucumber.

What's the difference between a terrorist and a woman with PMS?
You can negotiate with a terrorist.

Two guys are in shit up to their noses. One guy turns to the other and says, "We're gonna die."
The other guy asks, "Why?"
"Because I got diarrhea."

Why did the man have a $1,000 bill tattooed on his penis?
So, when his wife wanted to blow big money, she could do it at home.

What's a blonde's favorite nursery rhyme?
"Hump Me, Dump Me."

A doctor comes out of the examination room and says to the man waiting in the hallway, "I'm afraid I don't know whether your wife has Alzheimer's or AIDS."

The man asks, "What should I do, doc?"

"When you go home tonight, send her out for groceries. A dozen eggs, a loaf of bread, and a quart of milk. If she finds her way home and has the right groceries . . . DON'T fuck her."

What's the definition of trust?
Two cannibals having oral sex.

A little boy passes his parents' room during the night after getting a glass of water. Seeing what he thinks are his parents playing in bed, he shouts, "Oh boy, horsey rides. Can I have a horsey ride, Daddy?"

Relieved that the boy isn't asking more uncomfortable questions, the father lets the boy climb on his back.

Pretty soon his mom starts moaning, and the little boy says, "Hang on, Daddy. This is the part where the mailman usually gets thrown off."

What do women and condoms have in common? They spend more time in your wallet than on your dick.

**Why do women fart after they pee?
They can't shake it, so they blow
on it.**

Why did the blonde put condoms on
her ears?
She didn't want to get hearing AIDS.

**What's the difference between
a hooker, a lover, and your wife?
    A hooker says, "Faster, faster."
    A lover says, "Slower, slower."
    And your wife says, "I think I'll
paint the ceiling beige."**

Why was the blonde upset with her
driver's license?
Because she got an F in sex.

What are the three biggest lies told by
a cowboy?
   "I won this belt buckle."
   "The truck is paid for."
   "I was just trying to help the sheep over the
fence."

**What's the difference between anal sex
and a microwave oven?
A microwave won't brown your meat.**

What's a nymphomaniac's worst nightmare?
Meeting a guy with herpes and a 12-inch dick.

**What do you do if a pit bull humps your leg?
Fake an orgasm.**

How is a blonde like a hair dryer?
Turn her on, and she starts to blow.

One night Pinnochio's girlfriend says to him, "This stinks. Every time we make love, I get splinters."

So Pinnochio goes to Gepetto and asks him for help.

"Sandpaper, my boy. That's all you need."

A few days later, Gepetto asks Pinnochio, "So how are things with the girls?"

And Pinnochio replies, "Who needs girls?"

What are the signs of love, true love, and showing off?
Spitting, swallowing, and gargling.

**How do you recondition an aging hooker?
Stick a 10-pound ham up her twat and pull out the bone.**

Why don't women have trouble with hemorrhoids?
Because God made them the perfect asshole.

Why don't blondes converse during sex?
Their mothers told them never to talk with their mouths full.

Did you hear about the gay choir boy?
Choked on his first hymn.

A shy guy in a bar works up the courage to talk to a good-looking girl having a drink. "Hi, my name's Scott," he says.

She turns to him and screams at the top of her lungs, "No, I will not sleep with you!"

Stunned and mortified, he skulks back to his seat.

A little while later, the girl comes up to him. "I'm sorry about before," she tells him. "I'm a psychology student, and I'm studying how people react to embarrassing situations."

He looks at her, smiles, and screams, "What do you mean $200 for a blow job?"

Did you hear about the transvestite who had tits grafted onto his back?
If his ass holds out, he'll be a millionaire.

What's the definition of eternity?
The time between when you come and when she leaves.

A doctor says to his patient, "I've got good news and bad news. The good news is your penis is going to grow five more inches in length and two inches in circumference."

The patient says, "That's great. What's the bad news?"

"It's malignant."

Why is a blonde like a screen door?
Because, the more you bang her, the looser she gets.

What do you call a lesbian with fat fingers?
Well hung.

A woman getting married for the fourth time is ordering her wedding gown. "I want a white gown," she tells the tailor.

"Pardon me for being indelicate," he says, "but isn't this your fourth time down the aisle?"

"Yes," she replies. "But, believe it or not, I'm still a virgin. My first husband was a psychologist. He just wanted to talk about it. And my second husband was a gynecologist. He just wanted to look at it."

"What about your third husband?" asks the tailor.

"He was a stamp collector. God, I miss him."

What's the ultimate rejection?
When you're jerking off and your hand falls asleep.

What's the worst thing about being an atheist? You have no one to talk to when you're getting a blow job.

Why is a blonde like a railroad track?
Because she gets laid all over the country.

What's a lap dog?
An ugly woman who gives good head.

What did one lesbian frog say to the
other lesbian frog?
"Hey, we do taste like chicken!"

What do you call a hooker with a
runny nose?
Full.

What do you call a female clone?
A clunt.

Why do women have pussies?
So guys will talk to them at parties.

What do you call wearing a condom during anal sex? Brown-bagging it.

A construction worker came home and found his wife in bed with another man. So he dragged the man into his garage and stuck his pecker in a vise. He tightened the vise all the way, then took out the handle, making it impossible to open. He then pulled a hacksaw off the wall.

"Oh, my God, you're not going to saw my cock off, are you?" cried the man.

"No," said the construction worker. "You are. I'm setting the garage on fire."

What does an 80-year-old woman's snatch smell like?
Depends. . . .

Why did the blonde keep failing her driving test?
Every time the examiner opened the car door, she jumped in the back seat.

A little boy walked in on his parents having sex. "What are you doing, Mommy?" he asked her.

Thinking quickly, the mother answered, "Uh, I'm sucking the air out of Daddy, sweetheart."

"I don't know what good it'll do," said the boy. "Tomorrow the lady next door will just blow him up again."

How can you tell if you have a high sperm count?
Your girlfriend has to chew before swallowing.

How do you paralyze a woman from the waist down?
Marry her.

What did the blonde's left thigh say to her right thigh?
"Between the two of us, we can make a lot of money."

Why are women like frying pans?
You have to heat them up before you slip in the meat.

A carpenter phones his wife in a panic.
"Honey, I just sawed off my finger."
  His wife asks, "The whole finger?"
  "No, the one next to it."

What do you call a man without an asshole?
Divorced.

A blonde goes to the doctor. The doctor asks her, "Are you sexually active?"

"No," she answers, "I just lie there."

How can you tell if your girlfriend is fat?
She sits on your face, and you can't hear the stereo.

How can you tell if your girlfriend is really fat?
You have to roll over twice to get off of her.

What's the best thing about a blow job from your wife?
The 10 minutes of silence.

Why don't they let blondes swim in the ocean?
Because they can't get the smell out of the tuna.

Why don't married men eat pussy?
Beggars can't be chewers.

What's the first thing Adam did when he came upon Eve?
Wiped her off with a fig leaf.

What's the most useless thing on your grandmother?
Your grandfather.

What did the genie say to the really ugly girl?
"God, that was gross! Okay, now what's your second wish?"

A young couple are spending the weekend in a log cabin. The guy goes out to chop wood for the fireplace. When he comes in, he tells his girlfriend, "Gee, honey, my hands are freezing."

"Here, put them between my thighs to warm them up," she says.

A little later he goes out to chop some more wood. Again he comes back and tells his girlfriend, "My hands are really freezing."

"Well, here, put them between my thighs and warm them up."

Later that night he chops some more wood to last until morning. Again he comes in and says, "Wow, my hands are really, really freezing."

She looks at him and angrily shouts, "For Christ's sake, don't your ears ever get cold?"

What did the nun say to the priest who was teaching her how to swim?
"Father, will I really sink if you take your fingers out?"

This guy's drinking at a bar when a drunk comes in and goes right up to him. "Your mom is the best fuck in town," says the drunk.

Everyone expects a brawl, but the guy just ignores the drunk.

Undeterred, the drunk keeps going. "Your mother just sucked my cock, and it was sweet," he yells.

Still the guy ignores him.

The drunk gets right in his face and says, "I fucked her in the ass, and she loved it."

Finally, the guy can't take it anymore. He looks at the drunk and says, "Dad, would you please go home and sleep it off?"

What did the professor do for the girl having trouble with sex education?
He kept her after school and pounded it into her head.

Why did the proctologist use two fingers?
He wanted a second opinion.

What do your wife and your computer have in common?
You don't realize how important they are until they go down on you.

A hillbilly says to his cousin, "I sure would like to get into your pants."

"Why?" she asks.

"Because I just shit mine."

The Lone Ranger and Tonto were riding on the plains one day. They stopped, and Tonto jumped off his horse and put his head to the ground. "Hmm, buffalo come," said Tonto.

Amazed at his partner's ability, the Lone Ranger exclaimed, "Damn, you Indians are smart. How did you know that?"

Tonto replied, "Face sticky."

What do elephants use for tampons?
Sheep.

**What did one gay sperm say to
another gay sperm?
"How the hell are we supposed to
find an egg in all this shit?"**

Why do blondes get confused in the
ladies' room?
Because they have to pull their own
pants down.

**How do we know God is a man?
Because, if God were a woman,
semen would taste like chocolate.**

Why do farts smell?
So the deaf can appreciate them too.

**How can you tell if your roommate
is gay?
You can taste shit on his dick.**

Why do women need men?
Because vibrators can't
buy drinks.

How does a hillbilly know when her sister is having her period?
Her father's dick tastes bloody.

If storks bring babies, what bird brings blow jobs?
Swallows.

Why can't blondes count to 70?
They can never get past 69.

A man and a woman were celebrating their 25th wedding anniversary. As they retired to their bedroom and undressed, the woman asked her husband, "When you first saw me 25 years ago, what were you thinking?"

"I was thinking how I just wanted to fuck your brains out and suck your tits dry," he said.

"And what are you thinking now?" she asked.

"I was thinking it looks like I did a good job."

What do you get when you cross a rooster with a telephone pole?
A 30-foot cock that wants to reach out and touch somebody.

How do you get AIDS from a toilet seat?
By sitting on it before the guy still using it gets up.

What did the woman say to the mink?
"Who did you have to blow to get that coat?"

What does an old woman have between her breasts that a younger woman doesn't have? Her belly button.

Why are blondes so quiet during sex? Their mothers told them never to talk to strangers.

A guy says to his buddy, "Man, I was so drunk last night that I blew chunks."

"Big deal," says his buddy. "I do that all the time."

"You don't understand," says the guy. "Chunks is my dog."

What do a warm toilet seat and a blonde have in common?
You can't help but wonder who was there before you.

How do you circumcise
a hillbilly?
Kick his sister in the chin.

**Have you heard about the new
restaurant that prints the bill on a
condom?
That way a guy can wine and dine his
date and then stick her with the tab.**

What do spaghetti and a nymphomaniac
have in common?
They both wiggle when you eat them.

**What's the definition of indefinitely?
You know you're "in," "definitely,"
when your balls are smacking her ass.**

Did you hear about the new lesbian shoe called Dike?
It comes with an extra-long tongue, and you can get it off with one finger.

What do you call the layer of sweat between two hillbillies having sex? Relative humidity.

Why are women like laxatives?
They irritate the shit out of you.

An Eskimo's snowmobile breaks down, so he takes it to a mechanic. The mechanic looks it over and says, "I think you blew a seal."

"Nah," says the Eskimo, "that's just frost on my moustache."

What do a cobra and a three-inch dick have in common?
Nobody wants to fuck with either of them.

Did you hear about the sex maniac who went into taxidermy?
He would mount anything.

A woman sees a sign in a pet shop window that says "Pussy-Licking Frog Inside." She goes inside, and before she can say anything the guy behind the counter says, "Bonjour, madame."

What has 75 balls and fucks old ladies?
Bingo.

A little boy asks his father where babies come from, and his father says, "The stork."

The kid says, "Yeah, yeah, I know that, but who fucks the stork?"

Why are women like banks?
You deposit, you withdraw, you lose interest.

Sign on a whorehouse door: "Out to lunch. . . . Beat it."

A guy walks up to a pretty woman in a bar and asks her, "Do you know the difference between a chicken leg and a man's dick?"

"No," she replies.

"In that case, how'd you like to go on a picnic?"

Why does a blonde love it when her boyfriend uses a condom?
She has a doggy bag for later.

What's the definition of a perfect woman?
A deaf and dumb nymphomaniac whose father owns a beer store.

Did you hear about the woman who went fishing with seven guys?
The only thing she went home with was a red snapper.

What did the kid say after peeking into his parents' bedroom?
"Wow! And they sent me to a psychiatrist for sucking my thumb."

If a sheep is a "ram," and a mule is an "ass," how come a ram in the ass is a "goose"?

What's long and hard to a blonde?
Grade three.

A young woman set out to become rich by looking sharp and staying on her toes. She was able to look sharp, but she didn't get rich until she got on her knees.

Why do tampons have strings?
So you can floss after you eat.

What do you call sperm from a homosexual?
Fruit juice.

A little boy asks his father, "Dad, what does
wife-swapping mean?"
The father says, "Go next door and ask your
mother."

Two 90 year olds had been dating for a while
when the man told the woman, "Tonight's the
night we have sex." And so they did.

Afterward they were lying together in bed,
and the man thought to himself, "Man, if I'd
known she was still a virgin, I would have been
more gentle with her."

And the woman was thinking to herself, "My
God, if I'd known the old bastard could actually
get it up, I would have taken off my pantyhose."

Dwayne masturbates during porno films so much that his business card reads "Coming at a theater near you."

What do you do if your date says it's nice out?
Leave it out.

Why did the man divorce his blonde wife and marry a garbage can?
The hole was smaller and smelled better.

A father says to his son, "Son, you gotta stop jerking off, or you'll go blind."
The son says, "Dad, I'm over here."

What's totally confused and incredibly horny?
A blind lesbian in a fish market.

What do you have to do before entering the tunnel of love in San Francisco?
Dress up like a gerbil.

Who's the most popular man in a nudist colony?
The guy who can carry two coffees and a dozen doughnuts.

Who's the most popular woman in a nudist colony?
The one who can eat the last doughnut.

How do you know if your girlfriend's a slut?
You call her for phone sex, and she gives you an ear infection.

What's the difference between a blonde and a bowling ball?
You can fit only three fingers in a bowling ball.

A couple are making out when she asks him to put another finger in.

"What do you want to do?" he asks. "Whistle?"

What do you have if a mule eats the legs off a rooster?
Two feet of cock in your ass.

A guy is fucking his girlfriend in the ass when she tells him, "Stop. It hurts."

And he says, "Are you kidding? It feels great."

What's the best thing about a woman with a small hand? She makes your dick look bigger.

Three women talking about their boyfriends decide to nickname them after soft drinks. The first woman says, "I'm going to call my Donny 'Mountain Dew' because he's as big as a mountain and always wants to 'do' it."

The second woman says, "I'm calling my Bill '7-Up' because he's got seven inches and he's always up."

The third woman says, "I'm gonna call my Howard 'Jack Daniels.'"

The other women look at her. "But Jack Daniels is a hard liquor."

The third woman replies, "That's my Howard!"

What do you say to a blonde with no arms and no legs?
Nice tits.

What do you call the irritating part around a woman's pussy?
The woman.

**Why do men pay more for car insurance?
Because women don't get blow jobs while
driving.**

What does a perverted parrot say?
"Polly want a crack at 'er."

**How do you get a nun pregnant?
Dress her up like an altar boy.**

Did you hear about the perverted archaeologist?
He could sniff a used tampon and tell you what
period it came from.

**A blonde is fooling around with her date
when she says, "Could you take off your
ring? It's hurting me."
 And the guy says, "Ring, hell, that's my
wristwatch."**

Why do women prefer older gynecologists? Their fingers shake.

What's the difference between "oooooh" and "aaaaah"?
About three inches.

A woman goes to her gynecologist with a vibrator stuck in her twat.

The gynecologist tells her, "Don't worry, I'll have it out in a minute."

"Forget that," the woman tells him. "I just want you to replace the batteries."

Why is life like a penis?
Because when it's soft it's hard to beat, and when it's hard you get screwed.

How do you know God meant for men to eat pussy?
Why else would he make it look like a taco?

**What's the difference between
a hunting dog and a homosexual?
A hunting dog "sics" "ducks."**

What do you call a woman who can suck
a golf ball through a garden hose?
Darling.

**How is mountain climbing like getting
a blow job from an ugly woman?
Whatever you do, don't look down.**

What's a birth control pill?
The other thing a girl can put
in her mouth if she doesn't
want to get pregnant.

What do a plate of eggs Benedict and
a blow job have in common?
You can't get either one at home.

**Did you hear about the porno director
who demanded all his actors not be
circumcised?
He wanted to advertise the movie as
"totally uncut."**

A man on a date gets upset when she
starts ordering large amounts of the most
expensive items on the menu. "Do you
eat this much at home?" he asks her.

"No. But then nobody at home wants
to fuck me."

**Did you hear about the generic
condoms?
They're for cheap fuckers.**

A couple were engaged in foreplay when the woman said, "Why don't you make my pussy talk?"

"How do I do that?" asked her partner.

"Put a tongue in it."

What's worse than a piano that's out of tune in the morning?
An organ that goes flat in the middle of the night.

How do you make Maneschewitz wine?
Squeeze his balls.

Tits are a lot like electric trains.
They're meant for children, but dad always ends up playing with them.

A man had "I love you" tattooed on his penis. When his wife saw it, she screamed at him, "Quit trying to put words in my mouth!"

A man drags a woman into the bushes and starts molesting her. She yells out, "Help, help, I'm being robbed!"

The man says, "You ain't being robbed, you're being fucked."

She says, "Well, if this is what you call being fucked, I'm getting robbed."

How do you take revenge on a guy if you catch him screwing your wife?
Shoot his guide dog.

What's the difference between a stud and a premature ejaculator?
One is good for seconds; the other is only good for seconds.

Did you hear about the blind gynecologist?
He made his money reading lips.

A boy walks in on his mother and father having sex. The embarrassed parents tell the boy they're making him a sister. The next day the father sees the boy crying and asks him what's wrong. The boy says, "You know the little sister you were making for me? Today the mailman ate her."

Did you hear about the guy who went to the premature ejaculator's meeting?
He showed up an hour early.

Condoms now come in three sizes . . . small, medium, and liar.

How does a blonde turn on the light after sex?
She opens the car door.

What do tofu and a vibrator have in comon?
They're both meat substitutes.

They just invented a combination aphrodisiac and laxative.
Its slogan is "Easy come, easy go."

Did you hear about the unfortunate young man who was thrown out of Scouts?
They caught him eating Brownies.

What do you call an anorexic with a yeast infection?
A quarter pounder with cheese.

A man met a really cute girl and by their second date had forgotten whether she'd said she had TB or VD, so he phoned his doctor and asked what he should do. The doctor told him, "If she coughs, fuck her."

What did one ball say to the other?
"Why should we hang? It was dick who did all the shooting."

What's the difference between a hog and a man? A hog doesn't have to buy drinks all night so he can fuck some pig.

What's brown and has holes in it?
Swiss shit.

What do you get when you cross a donkey with an onion?
A piece of ass that brings tears to your eyes.

When you get married, there are three kinds of sex. The first is house sex, where you make love everywhere in the house. Next is bedroom sex, where you make love only in the bedroom. Finally, there's hall sex. That's where you pass each other in the hall and say, "Fuck you."

A blonde tried to rob a bank, but she got everything backward.
She tied up the safe and blew the guard.

**What's hard and stiff when you put it in and soft and sticky when you pull it out?
Chewing gum.**

What's the difference between a fox and a pig?
About six beers.

**What do you call a hooker's vagina?
A chamber of commerce.**

Did you hear about the basketball player
who married a midget?
He was nuts over her.

**What do you call a German tampon?
A twatstika.**

Did you hear about the Polack whose wife had
triplets?
He got a gun and went looking for the other
two guys.

**What's pink, moist, and split in the middle?
A grapefruit.**

What's the difference between looking for a lost
golf ball and Lady Godiva?
Looking for a lost ball is a hunt on a course.

81

Two girls are at the movies. One says to the other, "Oh no, the man next to me is masturbating."

Her friend tells her, "Just ignore him."

"I can't," she replies. "He's using my hand."

On their honeymoon night, the young bride said, "Now that we're married, you can teach me what a penis is."

The groom proudly opened his trousers and showed her.

"Oh, I see. It's like a prick, only smaller."

What's the difference between a Ritz and a lesbian?
One is a snack cracker, and the other is a crack snacker.

What's the quickest way to get into a blonde's pants?
Well, first you pick them up off the floor. . . .

What do you call a man from Copenhagen who's just had a circumcision?
A pruned Danish.

What's the definition of a vagina?
The box the penis comes in.

A new study says that 60% of homosexuals were born to their sexual persuasion . . .
and the other 40% were sucked into it.

What's the difference between an old cat and a kitten?
An old cat can scratch and claw, but a little pussy never hurt anyone.

Did you hear about the new all-woman delivery service? It's called UPMS.
They deliver whenever the fuck they feel like it, and you'd better not complain if it's late.

Why don't prostitutes ever vote in elections? Because they don't care who gets in.

What's the difference between a blonde and a limousine? Not everybody's been in a limousine.

A nymphomaniac is walking through the parking lot of her supermarket with the bag boy carrying her groceries. She leans over to him and whispers, "I have an itchy pussy."

The bag boy looks at her and says, "Well, you'd better point it out, lady, because I can't tell one Japanese car from another."

**Did you hear about the new morning-
after birth control pill for men?
You take it the next day, and it
changes your blood type.**

Why did Frosty the Snowman pull his
pants down?
He heard the snowblower coming.

**Did you hear about the whore who
went to work in a leper colony?
She was doing all right until her
business started dropping off.**

Why is a gynecologist like an incurable
gossip?
Because he spends a lot of time
spreading old wives' tails.

Where can a midget spend the night without paying?
A stay-free minipad.

Why did the gay guy run away from home?
He didn't like the way he was being reared.

How do you get five pounds of meat out of a fly?
Open my zipper.

One ovary said to the other ovary, "Did you order any furniture? There are a couple of nuts outside trying to shove an organ in."

Who was the world's first computer multitasker?
Eve. She had an apple in one hand and a wang in the other.

Did you hear about the redneck who thought a sanitary belt was drinking from a clean glass?

What do you call graffiti on men's room walls?
Squatter's "writes."

What's the difference between mononucleosis and herpes?
You catch mono from snatching kisses . . .
and you catch herpes by kissing snatches.

What does a married woman do with her asshole first thing in the morning?
She sends him off to work.

A man asked his local hooker if she'd give him one on credit. "No way," she said. "You're into me too much already."

There's only one thing prettier than a rose on a piano.
Two lips on an organ.

Bill's wife had a unique way to make love doggy style.
First she made him get down on all fours and beg . . .
and then she'd roll over and play dead.

Why are cab drivers such bad lovers? Because they never check to see if you're coming before they pull out.

A woman took the ashes of her recently departed husband to the top of a sky scraper and threw them into an oncoming gust of wind. "Here you go, sweetheart," she said. "There's that blow job I always promised you."

What did Mrs. Dumpty give to Humpty?
Egghead.

What do you get when you cross a hooker with a computer?
A fucking know-it-all.

Why don't blondes wear hoop earrings?
Because they keep getting their high heels caught in them.

What were the most erotic words ever spoken on television before 1960?
"Gee, Ward, you were kind of rough on the beaver last night."

Why doesn't Santa have any kids?
Because he comes only once a year, and
when he does it's down the chimney.

They just invented a new bra for girls with really
big tits.
They call it "The Sheepdog." It rounds them up
and points them in the right direction.

Why are pubic hairs curly?
So you don't poke your eyes out.

A man finds a bottle on the beach and discovers
a genie in it. The genie tells him, "For freeing me,
I shall grant you any wish."

"Great," says the guy. "I want to be rock hard
and get plenty of ass for the rest of my life."

POOF! The genie turns him into a toilet.

What's the difference between an ugly
girl and garbage?
Garbage gets taken out once a week.

**What two things in the air can lead to
a woman getting pregnant?
Her legs.**

A lady dwarf walks into a doctor's office and
says, "Doc, you gotta help me. Every time it rains,
I get a pain in my crotch."

The doctor tells her to get on the table. After
a few minutes of fiddling around, he tells her
he's done.

"Hey, I feel great," she says. "What did you
do?"

"I cut two inches off the tops of your galoshes."

**How does a whale perform oral sex?
It bites the end off a submarine and sucks
out the seamen.**

What's the difference between a trapeze act and
a beauty contest?
The trapeze act is a cunning array of stunts.

Two bums were walking down the street when they noticed a dog licking his balls. The first bum said, "Don't you wish you could do that?"
The second bum said, "Yeah, but I'm afraid he might bite me."

What's a hump?
A noun meaning the thing on the back of a camel, unless there's another camel on the camel's back. In that case, hump is a verb.

What do you call two gay lovers in an Irish pub?
Patrick Fits-Henry and Henry Fits-Patrick.

Why did the pedophile send $50,000 to Boys to Men?
He thought it was a delivery service.

Two sperm are swimming along when one of them asks the other, "How long till we get to the fallopian tubes?"
The other one answers, "It's gonna be a while. We just passed the tonsils."

What's the difference between a pickpocket and a peeping Tom?
A pickpocket snatches watches.

What does a man have in his pants that a woman doesn't want to get on her face?
Wrinkles.

What does a Polish bride get on her wedding night that's long and hard?
A new last name.

Why are alfalfa sprouts like
pubic hairs?
Most people just push them both
aside and keep on eating.

How did the teenage boy get a cracked
vertebra?
He was kissing his girlfriend on her front
porch when her father came out and
stepped on his back.

What's the first thing a sorority girl
does in the morning?
Put her clothes on and go back to
her dorm.

A lady is getting her first golf lesson. The pro tells her, "Just take the club like you would your husband's dick."

The woman does what the pro says and hits the ball right down the middle of the fairway.

The pro looks at the shot and says, "Beautiful. Nice shot. Now this time take the club out of your mouth, grab it with your hands, and we'll try for distance."

What's the difference between a genealogist and a gynecologist?
One looks up a family's tree, and the other just looks up the bush.

What does a blonde say after sex?
"So are you guys all with the same team?"

A man walks into a bar, notices the name tag on the waitress, and says, "Debbie. Nice name. What do you call the other one?"

What's the difference between a blonde and

a broom closet?
Only two men can fit inside a broom closet.

A lady asked her husband for a breast enlargement operation.

He told her, "We can't afford it. Why don't you try taking some toilet paper and wiping it between your breasts."

"Do you think that will work?" she asked.

"Why not?" he answered. "Look what it did for your ass."

What do you get if your girlfriend uses
a feminine hygiene spray?
Around-the-cock protection.

Why did the man make his wife go back to college?
He wanted to fuck a co-ed.

Why shouldn't you go down
on a 12-inch penis?
You might get
foot-in-mouth disease.

Why do rednecks prefer contraceptive sponges?
Because that way, after sex, their wives can get up and wash the dishes.

Why did God create women?
Because sheep can't cook.

Did you hear about the rancher's daughter who got a bad reputation?
She couldn't keep her calves together.

An Irish woman is rushed down to the brewery, where they tell her that her husband drowned in a vat of beer.

"Oh, my goodness," she cries. "Did he suffer?"

The foreman says, "I don't think so. He got out twice to piss."

How do you get a blonde to say no?
I don't know either.

Women are like toilets.
They're either taken or full of shit.

What's the definition of macho?
Getting circumcised with pinking shears.

A guy walks into a bar, orders six shots of whisky, and downs them one after the other.

The amazed bartender asks him, "Hey, buddy, what's the occasion?"

The guy says, "My first blow job."

"That's great," says the bartender. "Tell you what, have another one on me."

"No thanks," replies the guy. "If six didn't get the taste out, I don't think one more will help."

Why do women like playing Pac Man at the arcade?
Where else can you get eaten three times for 50¢?

Joe comes home from work. As soon as he walks in the door, his wife jumps on him, pulls down his pants, and starts blowing him.

He looks at her and says, "Okay, Linda, what did you do to the car?"

What comes after 69?
Listerine.

What was the young man's first clue that he had a small penis?
When his girlfriend went down on him, she didn't suck—she flossed.

A woman calls her gynecologist. "Doctor, did I forget my panties in your office?" she asks him.

"No, there are no panties here," he tells her.

"Thank you, doctor. I guess I left them at the dentist's."

You know a woman is paranoid when she puts a condom on a vibrator.

Did you hear about the couple who were ticketed for speeding while parked?
They were caught doing 69.

What do coffins and condoms have in common?
They both have stiffs in them.

What do you have when you're holding two green balls in your hand?
Kermit's undivided attention.

What did the elephant say to Adam?
"How do you breathe through that thing?"

A gynecologist is examining a woman. "My, you have a large vagina. My, you have a large vagina."

Angrily, the woman tells the doctor, "You didn't have to say it twice."

The doctor replies, "I didn't."

What's red and has seven dents in it?
Snow White's cherry.

What's the difference between true love and herpes?
Herpes lasts forever.

Johnny comes home and sees his mother masturbating and moaning, "I want a man. I want a man."

A few days later he sees her in bed with a man.

The next day Johnny's mother comes home and sees him rubbing his pecker while moaning, "Bicycle. Bicycle."

What do homosexuals call hemorrhoids?
Speed bumps.

What did the tampon say to the condom?
"If you break, we're both out of a job."

A woman enters the police station complaining about a virgin man who tried to rape her. The policeman asks her why she thought he was a virgin, and the woman replies, "Because I had to show him how to do it."

What's the difference between pink and purple?
Your grip.

**What do you get when you cross a blonde
with a mosquito?
I don't know, but it doesn't stop sucking
until it gets blood.**

How can you tell if your wife is dead?
The sex is the same, but the dishes start piling
up.

**A guy goes down on his wife and says,
"My, you're dry tonight, dear."
She says, "Honey, you're licking the rug."**

What's the difference between your job and your
wife?
After 20 years, your job still sucks.

Why do bald men cut
holes in their pockets?
So they can run their fingers
through their hair.

Did you hear about the guy who poured
six beers over his hands?
He wanted to get his date drunk.

**What happened when the streaker
ran up to three nuns?
The first nun had a stroke. The
second nun also had a stroke. But
the third nun didn't touch him at all.**

Whatt do you call a man with a broken
condom?
Daddy.

**What's the difference between
a pussy and a cunt?
A pussy is warm and inviting. A cunt
is the person who owns it.**

Two guys are talking about their wives in
bed, and the first guy says, "My wife acts
like a dog during sex."

"Sounds good," says the other guy.

"Not really," says the first guy. "She
keeps peeing on the rug."

**What should a girl bring if her
boyfriend invites her over for a bite?
Kneepads.**

What do you give the blonde who has
everything?
Penicillin.

**What do you call a blonde with a dollar
on her head?
All you can eat for under a buck.**

A poodle and a Doberman meet at the vet's. The poodle tells the Doberman, "I got so horny I fucked my mistress."

The doberman says, "So I guess you're here to get neutered like me?"

The poodle says, "No, I'm here for a mani-cure."

**Did you hear about the guy who went into
cloning?
His wife told him to go fuck himself.**

A 10-year-old boy tells his father that he wants to be just like him when he gets older.

The dad asks, "You mean a top salesman?"

The kid says, "No, I want to fuck Mom."

Did you hear about the moron who broke his leg on the golf course?
He fell off the ball washer.

A little girl was taken to the hair salon for the first time, and the hair dresser gave her a cookie. A few minutes later she started crying.

"What's the matter?" he asked. "Have you got hair on your cookie?"

She looked at him and said, "What are you, a pervert? I'm only six."

Farmer Ed catches his neighbor Bob banging his wife and grabs his shotgun. "Bob, you bastard!" he shouts. "I'm gonna blow your balls off!"

"C'mon, Ed, give me a chance!" screams Bob.

"Okay, I will," says Ed. "Swing 'em."

Why are blondes' coffins Y-shaped?
Because once they're on their backs their legs automatically open.

What do you call Raggedy Ann lying in the mud with a big stone in her mouth?
A dirty cotton rock sucker.

Why do little girls carry goldfish in their pockets?
To smell like big girls.

What did the blonde do when she heard the British were coming?
She stopped sucking.

What's the difference between hard and light?
You can still sleep with a light on.

Why did Helen Keller use two hands to masturbate?
One hand to do it and one hand to moan.

The young man asked his date, "If I try to make love to you, will you call for help?"
She replied, "Only if you need it."

A man bumps into his ex-wife and says, "What do you say we go back to my place and tear one off the way we used to for old time's sake?"

"Over my dead body," she replies.

He says, "Yeah, like I said, the way we used to."

What's the definition of burning love? When you reach for the Vaseline and pick up the Vicks instead.

What's the difference between a clitoris and a remote control?
A man won't stop looking until he finds the remote control.

What do you call a bikini bottom?
A gash mask.

What's the purpose
of a belly button?
It's a place to put your gum
on the way down.

What's the difference between a blonde
and an ironing board?
It's difficult to open the legs of an ironing
board.

**What did the Polack say when he
came home and found his best friend
on top of his wife?
"Down, Fido."**

Why don't blondes eat bananas?
They can't find the zippers.

What's the most tedious thing about banging
a blonde?
Waiting in line.

What's the definition of an overbite?
When you're eating pussy and it begins
to taste like shit.

A five-year-old girl is standing in front of a
supermarket smoking. A shocked old woman
asks her, "How long have you been smoking?"

"Since I had my first fuck," says the girl.

"Oh my!" says the old woman. "And when
was your first fuck?"

"I don't remember—I was drunk."

Did you hear about the version of Russian
Roulette for gays?
You pass around six boys, and one of them
has AIDS.

What do you get when you cross a Jehovah's Witness and a biker?
Someone who wakes you up at 7:30 on a Saturday morning and tells you to fuck off.

What do a gay prostitute and a lawyer have in common?
They both make a living fucking people up the ass.

A guy walks into a whorehouse, pulls down his pants, and proudly reveals an 18-inch cock.

The girl says, "You're not sticking that thing in me. I'll just suck it."

"Forget it," says the guy. "I can do that myself."

What do a tampon and a rich bitch have in common?
They're both stuck up cunts.

A Polish family is watching TV when the mother says to the father, "Let's S-E-N-D the K-I-D-S out B-A-C-K to P-L-A-Y . . . so we can fuck."

A bald guy and his date are making out hot and heavy when his toupee slides off. As he's groping around for it, his hand goes between her legs, up her skirt, and lands on her pussy.

"That's it! Oh, yes, that's it!" she cries.

"It can't be," he says. "I part mine on the side."

What do you call a blonde with a bag of sugar on her head? Sweet fuck all.

Which two words do you not want to
hear while standing at a urinal?
"Nice cock."

**What was the first commandment?
"Eve, suck my cock."**

What do you get when you cross a
blonde with a lawyer?
I don't know, but it sure enjoys fucking
people.

**Why don't women have brains?
They don't have cocks to put them in.**

What's the definition of "penis"?
A fibrous muscle, often found in women.

Why did the golfer want to be reincarnated as a lesbian?
So he could still eat cunt while also getting to hit off the ladies' tees.

Two lawyers walking down the street see a beautiful woman.

One lawyer points to her and says, "Let's fuck her."

The other lawyer looks at her, thinks for a moment, and asks, "Out of what?"

How does a blonde like to have her tummy tickled?
From the inside.

What's the difference between a cow and a lesbian feminist?
Ten pounds and a flannel shirt.

Why did the biker call his disobedient dog Herpes?
Because it wouldn't heel.

Did you hear about the homosexual who went missing?
His lover had them put a picture of the back of his head on milk cartons.

What does a woman put behind her ears to make her more attractive to men?
Her ankles.

How does a woman like her eggs in the morning?
Fertilized.

What's the definition of a cigar?
A breath freshener for people who eat shit.

A newlywed groom says to his wife, "Okay, honey, this'll be our system for bed. If you want to have sex, pull my dick once. If you don't want to have sex, pull my dick . . . 1,400 times.

What's a virgin hillbilly?
A girl who can outrun her brothers.

What's the difference between your ex-wife and a catfish?
One is a scum-sucking bottom feeder, and the other is a fish.

What's the difference between a blonde and a trampoline?
A man takes off his shoes before jumping on a trampoline.

Why is a hurricane like a failed marriage?
It starts out with a lot of sucking and blowing, and then your house is gone.

What song did the seven dwarfs sing when Prince Charming kissed Snow White and brought her back to life?
"Hi ho, hi ho, it's back to jerking we go."

How can you tell when a blonde loses her virginity?
When all the boys in her kindergarten class don't have their milk money.

Did you hear about the new pill that cures AIDS?
It's called Trinoassatol.

Why do rednecks do it doggie style?
So they can both watch wrestling.

How do you get four blondes on a chair?
Turn it upside down.

How can you tell if you're in a gay church?
Only half the congregation is on their knees.

What do Polish women and hockey goalies have in common?
They both use the same pads for three periods.

Why did the high school student get angry during the football game? His cheerleader girlfriend did the splits, and another student's class ring fell out.

How can you tell if a girl's had sex with an elephant?
She sits on a bar stool and sinks to the floor.

Why don't priests approve of condoms?
They get caught in the altar boys' braces.

The young groom asks his new bride how he was in bed after their first time.

"I hate to break it to you, honey, but I don't think you're very good."

That's crazy," says the groom. "How can you make a decision like that after only 30 seconds?"

What's a Yankee?
The same as a quickie, but a guy can do it alone.

What's the definition of a male chauvinist pig?
A man who hates every bone in a woman's body except his own.

What do you get when you cross a rooster with an owl?
A cock that stays up all night.

Why is being in the army like getting a blow job?
The closer you get to discharge, the better you feel.

One day four nuns are waiting in line at confession.

The first nun says, "Forgive me, Father, for I have sinned."

"How?" asks the priest.

"I looked at a man's private parts."

"Wash your eyes in the holy water," says the priest.

The second nun says, "Forgive me, Father, for I have sinned. I touched the private parts of a man."

"Well, then you must wash your hands in the holy water," says the priest.

Suddenly, he hears the third and fourth nuns fighting.

"What's going on here?" he asks them.

And the fourth nun says, "I'm not going to drink the holy water if she's going to sit in it."

What's the difference between a woman in church and a woman in the bathtub?
A woman in church has hope in her soul.

How do you know if your doctor is gay?
He inserts a suppository with his teeth.

What did the old man do when his wife told him to give her nine inches and make it hurt?
He fucked her three times and punched her in the nose.

How would you describe an ugly guy's love life?
Fist or famine.

What do you call a gay milkman?
A dairy queen.

How are women like a toilet seat?
Without the hole in the middle, they wouldn't be good for shit.

Why do crabs make such a handy snack?
Because you can eat them right out of the box.

Why did prehistoric man first walk upright?
To free his hands so he could jerk off.

Why did the blonde stop using the pill?
Because it kept falling out.

What's the first sign of AIDS?
A cock in your ass.

Did you hear about the charity that raises money for women who can't afford vibrators?
It's called Toys for Twats.

What do elephants use as vibrators?
Epileptics.

What did the blonde say when she woke up under a cow?
"What are you guys still doing here?"

Why did the little boy want his grand-mother to take him to the bathroom?
Because her hand shakes.

What did the lesbian say when she guided her girlfriend's tongue toward her clitoris?
"This bud's for you."

What should you do in case of fallout?
Re-insert and shorten your stroke.

How did the pygmy boxer win all his fights?
He'd fill his mouth with ice and cold-cock
his opponents.

How can you tell if a man grew up with sisters?
One of his eyes is shaped like a keyhole.

How can you tell when a blonde is wearing
pantyhose?
When she farts, her ankles swell.

A guy goes into a bar and says to a pretty girl he
sees there, "I sure would like a little pussy."
    She says, "So would I. Mine's as big as a
two-car garage."

What's a good sign your girlfriend is getting
fat?
Her last two gynecologists died from the
bends.

What's the difference between a blonde and the average man?
The blonde has a higher sperm count.

**Did you hear about the cook who got his dick caught in the dishwasher at work?
The manager fired them both.**

What's a hillbilly's idea of safe sex?
Tying the sheep's legs so it doesn't kick.

A woman was feeling horny, but all her husband wanted to do was read a book. Every once in a while, he would reach over and rub her pussy.

"If you don't want to fuck, stop teasing me," yelled his wife.

"I'm not teasing you," he said. "I'm wetting my fingers so I can turn the page."

Why was the egg so sad?
Because it got laid only once.

132

What did the blonde do when the batteries ran out in her vibrator?
Faked an orgasm out of instinct.

There's a new sexual position called "the rodeo." What you do is mount her from the back, reach around, grab her tits with both hands, and say, "These are almost as nice as your sister's." Then try to stay on for eight seconds.

What did one saggy boob say to the other saggy boob?
If we don't get some support soon, people are going to think we're nuts.

What do an order of Kentucky Fried Chicken and a woman have in common?
After you get past the firm breasts and juicy thighs, all that's left is a greasy box to put the bones in.

A man is sitting on his porch when his wife walks by.

"Geez, honey," he says to her, "your ass is getting as big as a barbecue grill."

Later that night he gets horny and rubs up to her.

She turns to him and asks, "Are you sure you want to fire up this big ol' grill for that little piece of meat?"

A teenage girl runs home and asks her mother, "Is it true what Jenny told me? Babies come from the same place boys put their penises?"

"Yes, dear, it's true," says her mother.

"But then, when I have a baby," cries the girl, "it'll knock my teeth out!"

What do you call a female midget who's nice and gives head?
Short, sweet, and to the point.

Mothers have Mother's Day, and fathers have Father's Day. What do single guys have?
Palm Sunday.

A man comes home from work one day to find his girlfriend at the front door with her bags packed and ready to leave.

The man asks, "Why are you leaving?"

She replies, "Word around the neighborhood is you're a pedophile."

He answers, "That's a pretty big word for a six year old."

This young couple are about to make out in the girl's house. Before they go into her room, she tells her boyfriend, "My sister is sleeping in the bottom bunk, and I don't want her to know what we're doing. So, when I say 'baloney,' it means push harder. When I say 'pastrami,' it means push softer."

So they get into bed and start having sex. The girl says, "Baloney, baloney, baloney." Then she says, "Pastrami, pastrami, pastrami."

This goes on for about half an hour when the girl's sister yells, "Will you two stop making sandwiches? You're getting mayonnaise all over me."

Why did they kick the midget out of the nudist colony?
He kept getting in everybody's hair.

Why did they name Bill Clinton's dog Buddy? Because nobody in the White House wanted to yell, "Come Spot!"

What does a blonde say after multiple orgasms?
"Way to go, team!"

Why is Viagra like Disneyland?
You have to wait an hour for a three-minute ride.

Two nuns are riding their bicycles down a street.
    One nun says, "I don't believe I've come this way before."
    The other nun says, "Me neither. Must be the cobblestones."

What's the difference between a blonde and a pair of sunglasses?
A pair of sunglasses sit higher on your face.

Why is having sex like riding a bike?
You have to keep pumping if you want to get anywhere.

What's the difference between a good girl and a bad girl?

   The good girl starts the day saying, "Good morning, God."

   The bad girl starts the day saying, "Good God, morning!"

What's blonde, brunette, blonde, brunette . . . ?
A blonde doing cartwheels.

What's the difference between a fat woman and an old maid?
One is trying to diet, and the other is dying to try it.

What do you get when you cross a disobedient dog with a rooster?
A cock that won't come.

What did the blonde's boyfriend call her ears?
Love handles.

Did you hear about the guy who went to a costume party without a shirt and shoes?
He was a premature ejaculator. He just came in his pants.

A blonde walks into a drugstore and asks the clerk if he sells extra-large condoms.

"Yes, we do. Would you like to buy some?"

"No," she replies. "But if you don't mind, I'd like to wait around until someone does."

How can you tell when an auto mechanic just had sex? One of his fingers is clean.

Little Johnny is in class when the teacher says, "Can anybody give me an example of a multisyllable word?"

Little Johnny puts his hand up. "I know one, Miss Conners. Masturbate."

Embarrassed, the teacher smiles and says, "My, Johnny, that's a mouthful."

Little Johnny says, "Oh no, Miss Conners, you're thinking of a blow job."

A hillbilly was bragging to his buddy about his sexy girlfriend. "She has a clit like a pickle," the hillbilly said.

"That big?" asked the buddy.

"That sour."

An 80-year-old virgin gets an itch in her crotch, so she goes to the doctor.

"Sounds like crabs to me," the doctor tells her.

The old lady says, "But it can't be—I'm a virgin."

So the doctor examines her closely. "Well, I'll be damned. You don't have crabs," he says. "Your cherry rotted, and you have fruit flies."

A man dies and goes to hell. Satan greets him and shows him three doors. "Whichever door you pick," says Satan, "you'll switch with whoever is in there."

Behind the first door is a guy being whipped. Behind the second door is a guy being poked with a branding iron. Behind the third door is a guy being given a blow job by a beautiful girl.

"I'll take the third door," says the man.

"Fair enough," says Satan. He taps the beautiful girl on the shoulder. "You can go now, sweetie. I got a replacement for you."

A man snuggles up to his wife in bed and starts necking.

"Not tonight, honey," says his wife. "I have a gynecologist appointment tomorrow, and I want to be, you know, fresh."

The husband reluctantly turns over and tries to sleep. After a few minutes, he nudges his wife. "Do you have a dentist appointment tomorrow also?"

What are the three words you dread hearing the most when you're making love? "Honey, I'm home."